114943707

FIRETALKING

by

Patricia Polacco

photographs by

Lawrence Migdale

 Richard C. Owen Publishers, Inc.
Katonah, New York

Meet the Author titles

Verna Aardema *A Bookworm Who Hatched*
Jean Fritz *Surprising Myself*
Paul Goble *Hau Kola Hello Friend*
Lee Bennett Hopkins *The Writing Bug*
James Howe *Playing with Words*
Rafe Martin *A Storyteller's Story*
Patricia Polacco *Firetalking*
Cynthia Rylant *Best Wishes*
Jane Yolen *A Letter from Phoenix Farm*

Text copyright © 1994 by Patricia Polacco
Photographs copyright © 1994 by Lawrence Migdale

Richard C. Owen Publishers, Inc.
P.O. Box 585
Katonah, New York 10536

Library of Congress Cataloging-in-Publication Data

Polacco , Patricia .
    Firetalking / by Patricia Polacco ; photographs by Lawrence
Migdale .
      p . cm . — (Meet the author)
    ISBN 1-878450-55-7 : $12.95
    1 . Polacco , Patricia — Biography — Juvenile literature . 2 . Women
authors , American — 20th century — Biography — Juvenile literature .
3 . Children's stories — Authorship — Juvenile literature .
[1 . Polacco , Patricia . 2 . Authors , American . 3 . Women — Biography .]
I . Migdale , Lawrence , ill . II . Title . III . Series : Meet the author
(Katonah , N . Y .)
PS3566 . 0396Z464   1994
813 ' . 54 — dc20
[B]   93-48162

The text type was set in Caslon 540.
Editor-in-Chief/Art Director Janice Boland

Printed in the United States of America

9 8 7 6 5 4 3 2 1

To my family

I was born on July 11, 1944, in Lansing, Michigan,
and grew up in Union City until my parents divorced.
Then my mother, my brother Richard, and
I moved to Oakland, California.
Every summer, though, Richard and I went back
to Michigan to live with our dad.

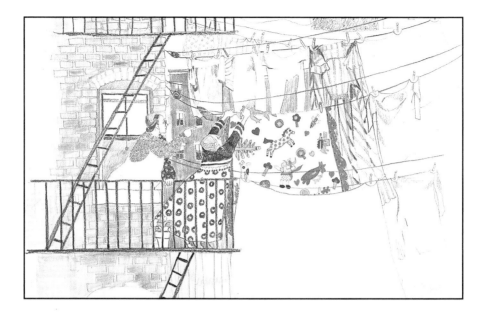

6

My mother's people were Russian
and my father's people were Irish.
In *The Keeping Quilt*, I tell how my mother's family
came to be here in America.
I still use this same wonderful quilt for
wedding chuppas, table cloths for special occasions,
and to welcome new babies into the world.
Both sets of my grandparents
were captivating storytellers.
With almost no urging at all
they squinted up their eyes,
watched our faces, and began to "tell".

Many of our evenings were spent in front
of the fireplace,
popping corn, eating apple wedges,
and hearing rich, incredible tales.
My babushka (my Ukrainian grandmother)
called this "firetalking".
Whenever she finished one of her tales of magic
and mystery, my brother and I would always ask,
"Bubby, is that a true story?"
She would look at us and reply, "Of course it's true…
but it may not have happened."

It was she who taught me to make
beautiful, decorated, *Pysanky* eggs.
Because I have such a special love for these Ukrainian eggs,
I wrote a story about them called *Rechenka's Eggs*.

My summers with my dad are golden memories.
He was a traveling salesman
and was on the road a lot.
But when Richard and I were with him,
he took time off to be with us.
We went fishing, took long walks in the woods,
and spent almost every other waking hour
on horseback.
He raised horses and took delight in teaching me
their secrets and noble ways.

Our school year was spent here in Oakland with my mom.
Her house was always filled with beautiful music
and lovely things to look at and touch.

She saw to it that I took ballet
and studied art and drama.
I loved it when she framed my drawings
and hung them up in the house.

In both Mom's house and at Dad's place
there was always a rocking chair, just for me.
I spent hours and hours
just rocking and dreaming every day.
I spent a lot of time in my imagination.
It soothed the pain of not doing well in school.

I had difficulty reading.

Math was and still is almost impossible for me.

I knew that inside I was very smart, but at school
I felt stupid and slow.

I had to work very hard to learn things.

Now that I am grown up I realize that I process
information differently than most people do.

My brain scrambles images that my eyes see.

But once I got the hang of it, I went on in school.

I even ended up graduating from college,
and getting my Ph.D. in Art History.

I didn't start writing and illustrating children's books
until I was 41 years old!
Before that I was busy being a wife, a mother,
and working for museums restoring ancient icons.
I am still a mother of a daughter and a son.
They are grown up now
and don't live with my husband and me.

My husband Enzo is a chef.
He spends most of his time giving cooking classes,
working in his butcher shop, and writing food reviews
for magazines and newspapers.
I met him in Australia when I was going to school.
Enzo is an Italian Jew from Trieste, Italy.
His people came to Italy from Poland.
Our name "Polacco" means
"that Polish man" in Italian.
Many members of his family died
in death camps during World War II.
I honor them by using their name, Polacco,
on my books.

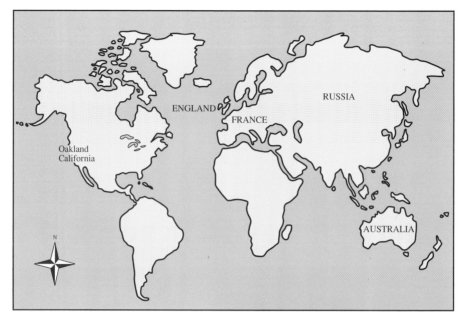

I have lived and studied in Australia, England, France, and Russia. Yet here I am, back in my beloved Oakland, California!

Patricia Polacco

Mrs. Katz and Tush

Enzo and I have three cats, Nina, Lo Lo, and Nikita.

Our most beloved cat, Tush, died last year, and she is now buried in a place of honor in our yard.

Dear little Tush inspired me to write *Mrs. Katz and Tush*.

17

We live in a very old, brown, shingle house
right in the center of town,
in the Rockridge District of Oakland.
Our yard has so many trees in it
people say they can't see our house!
Even though we are in the city,
it feels like the country.
What I love most about my neighborhood
are my friends and neighbors.
You can meet some of them in my books.

Chicken Sunday is a story
straight from my neighborhood.
Stewart Washington and his family
have been my neighbors for almost 31 years.
He is my best friend,
and we see each other almost every day.
We love to sit and talk on the porch together.

My family appears in my books, too.
Our son Steven is a graduate student in college
and is a very gifted artist.
Our daughter Traci lives in Washington
and is going back to school
to finish a degree in special education.

My mother lives a short walk from me in the house
that I grew up in.
She collects geodes and rocks,
probably because she saw a meteor land
in her front yard when she was very little.
I wrote *Meteor* to share that incredible event
with all of you.

The big one that landed in my mother's yard
is now our family headstone
in Riverside Cemetery in Union City, Michigan.
In our family we believe that if we touch it
and make wishes on it, the wishes come true.
I take a piece of that meteor to schools with me
and invite kids to wish on it!

I see my mother almost every day.
She was a classroom teacher for 38 years.
She loves cats, too.
Her cat, Miss Chiff,
loves being naughty
and getting into just about everything.

I am lucky... so very lucky!
I love my life.
Can you imagine doing what you love every day?
When I am working on a book,
I work every day until it is finished.
The first thing I do in the morning, though,
just like I did when I was a little girl,
is sit and rock.
I listen to music and let my imagination soar.
I take rocking so seriously I have at least
one or two rockers in every room in my house!

When I rock, my thoughts boil in my head.
They catch the air and fly.
The images and stories come with fury and energy.
I feel like Appelemando in *Appelemando's Dreams*.
My stories float above me!
I jot thoughts and outlines down on a pad,
then go out and do a run.

Running is something
I started doing about eight years ago
when my son was diagnosed with diabetes
and needed to exercise.
I used to run beside his bike to make sure
that he didn't have an insulin reaction.
After a while, he didn't need me anymore,
but I liked running so much I kept at it.
After my run, the work day begins.
I spend the next few hours talking on the phone,
typing, or drawing.

My heart sings whenever I am drawing.
As far back as I can remember,
I knew that drawing connected me somehow
to the universe and maybe even to God.
When I do illustrations for a book,
I first draw everything in pencil.
I make what is called a "rough dummy".
It looks exactly like the finished book,
except it's in black and white.

I use those drawings to make the "color finishes". I draw the layout in pencil, then I "lay in" the color with markers, acrylic paint, oil paint, pastels, and inks.

Sometimes I cut out photographs of real people
and paste them into my artwork.
I can't tell you how many
times I have made
my family, my friends, and
even my neighbors
stop what they were doing
to pose for me.
I don't always get my
drawing or stories right the
first time!
Sometimes I have to do
them over and over again!

Some days I go to schools and give author programs.
Sometimes I fly to other cities
to talk to children, teachers, and librarians.
As much as I love meeting children everywhere,
I always look forward to coming home.
I like to end a good, hard day,
sitting with my friends and family
in front of the fireplace.
One of us, and it never matters who,
will launch into a glorious tale told from the heart.
After the "firetalking," a small voice
will always ask, "Is that a true story?"
The answer is, "Of course it's true…
but it may not have happened."

Other books by Patricia Polacco

Uncle Vova's Tree; Babushka Baba Yaga; Just Plain Fancy; Picnic at Mudsock Meadow; Some Birthday; The Bee Tree; Thunder Cake.

About the Photographer

Lawrence Migdale took the beautiful photographs for this book. He lives with his wife Terry and son Daniel in Orinda, California.

Craig Morey

Acknowledgments

Photographs on pages 4, 10, 11, 12, and 13 appear courtesy of Patricia Polacco. Illustration on page 6 from *The Keeping Quilt* copyright © 1988 by Patricia Polacco, reprinted by permission of the publisher Simon & Schuster Books for Young Readers. Illustration on page 8 from *My Rotten Red Headed Older Brother* copyright © 1994 by Patricia Polacco used by arrangement with Simon & Schuster Books for Young Readers, a trademark of Simon & Schuster. Illustration on page 9 from *Rechenka's Eggs*, copyright © 1988 by Patricia Polacco; permission granted by Philomel Books, a division of The Putnam & Grosset Group. The book cover on page 17 from *Mrs. Katz and Tush*, copyright © 1992 by Patricia Polacco, permission granted by Bantam Books, a division of Bantam Doubleday Dell Publishing Group, Inc. Illustration on page 19 from *Chicken Sunday*, copyright © 1992 by Patricia Polacco, permission granted by Philomel Books, a division of The Putnam & Grosset Group. Illustration on page 25 from *Appelemando's Dreams*, copyright © 1991 by Patricia Polacco, permission granted by Philomel Books, a division of The Putnam & Grosset Group. Photograph on page 32 appears courtesy of Craig Morey.